Gigi Star

& Her Vocal Cords of Magic

By Kit Sinclair

Published by Playdead Press 2022

© Kit Sinclair 2022

Kit Sinclair has asserted her rights under the Copyright, Design and Patents Act, 1988, to be identified as the author of this work.

A CIP catalogue record for this book is available from the British Library.

ISBN 978-1-915533-05-0

Caution
All rights whatsoever in this play are strictly reserved and application for performance should be sought through the author before rehearsals begin. No performance may be given unless a license has been obtained.

This book is sold subject to the condition that it shall not by way of trade or otherwise, be lent, resold, hired out, or otherwise circulated without the publisher's prior consent in any form of binding or cover other than that in which it is published and without a similar condition including this condition being imposed on the subsequent purchaser.

Playdead Press
www.playdeadpress.com

Gigi Star and her Vocal Cords of Magic opened at Applecart Arts September 5th 2022. It originated after Kit Sinclair was an artist in residence with Applecart Arts in 2021 where a work in progress live stream took place.

Creative Team

Writer and Performer	**Kit Sinclair**
Composer and Performer	**Tom Blake**
Director	**Charlotte Ive**
Producer	**Rebecca Prentice**
Lighting Designer	**Will Adler**
Creative Caption Designer	**Edalia Day**
Illustrator and Set Designer	**Charlotte Ive**
Videographer	**Erica Belton**
Technical Stage Manager	**Rebecca Prentice**
Social Media Manager	**Saskia O'Hara**
Sound Designer	**Tom Blake**
Creative Consultant/Dramaturg	**Hetty Hodgson**

Supported by Arts Council England and Applecart Arts.

This script was written with generous support from the Peggy Ramsey Foundation.

Kit Sinclair

Kit Sinclair is a multi-award-winning performer and writer. She recently won the international Nancy Dean playwriting award. Her acting credits include; *EastEnders, Casualty*, and ITV's *Inspector Lewis*. As a writer, she is currently under commission for Hampstead Theatre having recently finished their Inspire program mentored by Roy Williams.

She was also on the Kiln Artists Development program and a Soho Theatre Alumni writer. Kit's solo show *'Awakening'* completed a highly successful run at the Underbelly, Edinburgh Fringe Festival where it was listed as a Lyn Gardner top pick. Her short film *'Aeroplanes'* (directed by Cannes winner Paul Shammasian) screened at festivals worldwide including BAFTAs Underwire festival where Kit was nominated for 'Best Actor'.

Tom Blake

Tom Blake is an actor, musician and composer. He trained at Ecole Philippe Gaulier, France. Before working as an actor he studied visual art at the Slade School of Fine Art, making work as a painter and performance artist. Previous work includes *Gods and Dogs* (The Rude Mechanical Company), *The Open* (The Space), *It Will Make You Feel Better* (Theatre 503), *Stop and Search* (Arcola Theatre) and *Not Helping* (Stockwell Playhouse) in a production that won the annual One Act Play Festival. Tom will be featuring in upcoming Sony Pictures film *It's All Coming Back to Me*.

With special thanks to:

Catriona Sinclair and Peter Osmon | For always supporting me. Forever holding me and encouraging me to carry on even when I can't see the light. I am eternally grateful.

Becca Prentice | You are extraordinary and I am so lucky to know you and love you.

Tom Blake | For making the most beautiful music and for pushing me to create a better script.

Charley Ive | For the incredible drawings and for being such a fun director. Your creativity knows no bounds.

Will Alder | For making this play look ridiculously beautiful and for knowing everything there is to know about tech.

Louse Ripley-Duggan | For reading all my ridiculous work and believing in it.

Giorgi Young | for the excellent photos

Shannon Latoyah Simon, Sam Taylor & Annie Kershaw | For the early days of this piece. Without that work in progress this wouldn't exist.

Ella Platts | For being my biggest hype woman and always buying tickets for my shows first

Erica Belton, Peter Moreton, Edalia Day, all the applecart cafe staff for endless cups of tea and coffee, Estelle Bingham, Steve Lane, Karen Prentice-Lawson, Denis Lawson, Hugo Timbrell, Brett Sherriffs, all the staff at Hampstead Theatre but an extra special shout out to Hannah Fischer and Chloe Burton for saving us when we needed ridiculous amounts of tech!

For

Fiona Sinclair – finally not a miserable play xxx

The show should be underscored with live music throughout. The first show used: a saxophone, an electric guitar, an acoustic guitar and two mics on stands, however this is open to interpretation.

Hanging from the ceiling are various household objects, things which make noise and can replicate musical instruments. For example: wind chimes, a sauce pan, a triangle. These are hit to symbolise a scene change.

The set should be representative of a 'junkyard in space'.

GIGI: It's 3:33am. The world sleeps

DOUBT: Just not here.

GIGI: This is London, which is basically New York City just on less steroids

DOUBT: If you've come hoping to see a show about positivity and manifesting then we suggest you leave

GIGI: I'd rather they didn't actually. Need the money

DOUBT: It's always about the money... You're no doubt assuming this show is about two separate characters... Well, you're wrong. This isn't my show. This isn't *my* story

GIGI: It's mine

DOUBT: Gigi Star

GIGI: And right now, he's also me

DOUBT: Kind of

GIGI: He's significant but not exactly the heart and soul. More like the brittle edges. What you might call my inner monologue of Doubt. The one which runs riot and ruins your chances of being present, confident –

DOUBT: And happy

GIGI: He hasn't always existed. He just sort of turned up one day and continued to grow. Like a fungus

DOUBT: It was the day you contracted bed bugs from the Overground and took them back to the warehouse you lived in. I saw an opportunity to thrive, and I took it.

GIGI: It's 3:37 am. I'm wide awake in my 'cosy' bedroom in an over-priced, shitty shared warehouse. Somewhere between Hackney and London Fields

DOUBT: Because she's a cliché

GIGI: Not a cliché, relatable…

DOUBT: Gigi's belly rumbles in rhythm with the out-of-tune psychotic city birds

GIGI: Which are currently upside down and eating each other – belly first

DOUBT: They don't know which way is up thanks to the 24-hour neon lights which flood their beady eyes.

GIGI: My room is a prison cell I pay to stay in. I'm not one for self-pity –

DOUBT: Yes, you are –

GIGI: But this isn't quite the life I had envisioned. Late twenties, living in a shithole staring at a poster of a window on my wall, because the room with the window was out of my price range

DOUBT: Should have moved south of the river then

GIGI: The view from this "window poster" is of the swirly milky way. Not the chocolate bar, the galaxy

DOUBT: No, not that chocolate either. That magical world which hangs above us and dictates so much of our behaviour.

GIGI: My existence is a bit grim actually

DOUBT: Which is why we've got to go back

GIGI: I'm not starting the show again

DOUBT: 27 years back

GIGI: Oh, fun. I like this bit

DOUBT: Course you do. It was kinder times, and I wasn't around. You were nothing but a speck of opportunity in the womb

Music cuts out.

GIGI: What you done that for?

DOUBT: I don't exist in this bit. Think I'll sit it out

GIGI: Are you seriously taking a break?

Unbelievable

Doubt is plunged into darkness

GIGI: November 21st. My parents never anticipated me being a Scorpio-Sagittarius cusp
They're in for rough ride
A lightning bolt similar to Bowie's makeup,
Shakes up the hospital,
in what appears mythological
As I come out fist held high like Freddie Mercury,
Lungs belting,
But not with cries
With lullabies:

I have to believe,
This passion which burns inside
Will conquer not divide
I'm destined to rise
I'm here to voice my words, worldwide

Everyone in the local hospital of Hummel Doddie halts.
Transfixed in some magical stupor
"I've never heard anything like it." Midwife Maureen murmurs
"She's born to be a star"
So, they call me 'Gigi' meaning 'Earth's worker'
Because my life's purpose is set
The silhouette to my future pre-decided

And they call me 'Star' because that is my surname.
My dad, an avid astrologer, works out my chart
"For a start, we've got a problem,
Scorpio sun, Cancer moon and Leo rising
Which is unsurprising given she's destined for the stage."

Doubt interjects

DOUBT: Absolute shit show of a chart to be honest.

GIGI: I'm admired by all five hundred occupants of Hummel Doddie
A forgotten sleepy, seaside town with a melancholy demeanour
I perform to make life less small and dull in small and dull village
I run up and down Hummel Doddie's humpy howie backstreets.
Everyone calls me 'the girl with the 'Vocal Cords of Magic'
They say life here is better with me in it.

Music and lights back up to reveal Doubt

DOUBT: So naturally she leaves.

DODDIE 1: "Don't forget us!"

DODDIE 2: "Do Hummel Doddie proud!"

DODDIE 3: "You're a star, Gigi!!"

GIGI: Waving me off, four whole years ago… Was it really four years?

DOUBT: There was a pandemic in the middle

GIGI: Let's not

DOUBT: No. Let's not.

Back to present day

GIGI: It's 4:44 am. Those hopeful but distant voices haunt me

DOUBT: Gigi cries, alone, as she always does

GIGI: London is transient, it's hard to make human friends.

DOUBT: Her salty tears awaken Pippin

GIGI: The dormouse who lives in my pocket. Pippin exclusively wears three-piece suits and high-top trainers thrifted second-hand. He's a TikTok sensation, with a side hustle on OnlyPaws. Despite his celebrity, his earnings aren't enough to get us out of this hell hole. He lives in my pocket because I think, he loves me. He's also a big fan of the E8 postcode with all its bougie artisan coffee shops

PIPPIN: Psst, Gigi

GIGI: Yes Pippin

PIPPIN: Have things started getting weird yet?

DOUBT: Here it comes

GIGI: The wallpaper starts to spin

DOUBT: Clockwise or anti-clockwise?

GIGI: My sinews are shifting.
My cells morphing.
This cupboard of a room is distorting.
As the arms on my clock begin to do the hopscotch,
As the planets above begin to sway and rock.
I feel like I'm tripping balls.

DOUBT: Those are the rules.

GIGI: The rats which inhabit my walls begin to bark!

DOUBT: Well, this is a lark

GIGI: I can't believe this is happening ….

DOUBT: Course it is, Gigi. Your Saturn is Returning.
According to the stars it's steep learning ahead.
Saturn's Return happens to us all

GIGI: Pippin, hold tight

DOUBT: It's that tussle of time when we must leave youth behind and enter adulthood

GIGI: I don't want to

DOUBT: Fine, join the 27 club then.

GIGI: I definitely don't want to do that

DOUBT: Think of it like puberty but worse. Every 27 to 29 years, Saturn returns to the exact point it did when you were born… And things get freaky.

GIGI: Outside the urban foxes dance the foxtrot as they discuss the stock market

DOUBT: Those sneaky foxes

GIGI: The reality of my world which was already a bit skewed is starting to feel... Extra freaky. I would like to scratch my eyeballs out

DOUBT: Please don't. Don't fancy a trip to A&E

GIGI: I chewed off my nails in a fit of anxiety and now my cuticles are dripping glitter down my forearm

Glitter drips down Gigi's arm

What if I'm next in line to join the 27 club?

DOUBT: I don't think these capitalist creatures know what that is, Gigi.

GIGI: Then tell them before everything goes upside down and inside out!

DOUBT: Tonight, three lost souls were given envelopes. Congratulations, your nanosecond of fame has come. Audience member one – please open:

ONE: Kurt Cobain

DOUBT: RIP – cut the cord of life aged 27. Number two - open:

TWO: Amy Winehouse

DOUBT: RIP – Vacated planet earth aged 27. Number three – open:

THREE: Jimi Hendrick

DOUBT: RIP – Kissed the stars aged 27! Better not make the dead angry, Gigi. Best mention the others.

GIGI: Oh, okay, erm- Janis Joplin

Weird game host noise

        Jim Morrison

Weird game host noise

        Jade Goody

Weird game host noise

        Some things really are written in the stars.

DOUBT: And something major is about to happen outside of Gigi's control.

Gigi looks panicked.

GIGI: It's 7:17 am. I lick my receipts to make sure I really get my money's worth, and I head to work

DOUBT: Gigi Star, in her Primarni ill-fitting pencil skirt and musty shirt sits hunched in her work cubicle. A piece of her soul dies with each cold call:

GIGI: "Hello. Have you had an accident that wasn't your fault?"

Dead dial tone sounds

        "Due to unpaid tax, our records indicate there's a warrant out for your arrest"

Dead dial tone sounds

> "This job is rotting my insides and my boss is a fucking moron."

DOUBT: Too late, they've already hung up like they always do.

GIGI: I must seek joy where I can... I shorten my boss's name "Hi, Dick!" His name is Ian.

DOUBT: Dick is a lizard in a suit. He wears crocodile shoes and snakeskin shirts. To honour his reptilian ancestors.

GIGI: I spit in his tea

DOUBT: You sick fuck

GIGI: I've gotta get my kicks somewhere... I've tried everything to break into the music industry

DOUBT: Mix tapes to producers, started a Youtube channel

GIGI: Read 'How to be TikTok famous' – Don't bother

PIPPIN: Gigi, you can't manipulate the algorithm. I just got lucky. Besides, it's all a load of tosh anyway

GIGI: And yet all anyone cares about is how many followers I have

STAPLER: Oi! You!

GIGI: Why is my stapler speaking?

STAPLER: Attention! Get yourself in line, Private Star… Nothing comes for free you entitled little rat bag. You've got to earn your place. Where's your stamina? Where's your discipline? The world doesn't need more pop stars. I say get up, work harder and stop moaning you stinking little snowflake! Now drop down and give me ten you big, fat FAILURE or I'll staple / that miserable mouth of yours shut.

GIGI: / Sod this. I drown the judgmental stapler in the staff toilet

DOUBT: And she sulks because in her eyes and in the stapler's eyes-

GIGI: I am a big fat failure

DOUBT: She's given her all to this city which feeds on dreams but nourishes nothing. It's as if her magical vocals don't work here…

GIGI: The office floor twists and turns like a merry-go-round. I've gotta get out of here

DOUBT: Relieved to be leaving her day box. She travels in a tube-shaped box, to get to a bigger box, where people escape from watching the box-

GIGI: Stop talking about boxes!

DOUBT: But all they do is stare at the box in their hands and drink from a…. *(Actor encourages audience to say box stand up style)*… Cylinder.

GIGI: Doubt, I need you to behave now. It's time

DOUBT: For what?

GIGI: My weekly open mic slot. The floor feels sticky. I hope that's cider

DOUBT: It's piss

GIGI: ...

Gigi steps forward ready to sing. The voices of Hummel Doddie ring in her ears

DODDIE 2: "Do Hummel Doddie proud!"

DODDIE 3: "You're a star, Gigi!!"

GIGI: This jungle city, built from concrete crumbles
Beneath me,
"Perhaps you needed to be humbled"
Whispers the shadow self as I tumble
Like loose change out a pocket.
Desperately wishing a rocket
Would stir everybody up.

Awaken the masses
Cuz we're walking with our feet stuck in
Molasses
Getting nowhere.
Maximum effort, minimum return.
Where the people in power don't seem concerned
That the oceans are on fire
Our government is fronted by a liar,
The reality is we're living in a satire.
Our human rights bound by barbed wire.

I'm clutching for dear life
Tugging at coat tails
Feeling like I've failed
Before I've even started.
This industry ain't for the fainthearted
I knew that, but naivety assumed that
Talent out weighted mediocrity.
Turns out it's just a hypocrisy.

I don't mean to sound bitter
But am I just a gravedigger
With a shovel full of purpose?
Burying it six feet under
No wonder I'm raging like thunder....

Got me questioning,
What if I wasn't a She
Would managers then want me?
Am I forever tied to a patriarchy,
Who desire voiceless femme fatales.
Just silent vessels to nestle more fatherless children.

So perhaps the daughter of an astrologist
Threatens the misogynists.
But I have to believe,
This passion which burns inside
Will conquer not divide.
I'm destined to rise
I'm here to voice my words, worldwide.

Gigi eyeballs the audience

    Is it me or does the audience look a little…?

DOUBT: Unhinged?

GIGI: There's a naked woman in the front row covering her bits in leaves. There's two giant lions in the middle and a man crawling with crabs

DOUBT: Maybe he has crabs

GIGI: Do you have crabs?

DOUBT: On reflection, I think you might be seeing them as their star signs, Gigi

GIGI: That makes sense. Either way, it's a small audience

DOUBT: Always is

GIGI: I'm losing faith here. I'm never going to make it performing to a room of ten people. Did all five hundred occupants of Hummel Doddie, bullshit me?

DOUBT: Is she in fact just a little bit crap? Her dream of global success looking unlikely… Gigi, glance to your left

Gigi looks left

GIGI: Okay don't all turn at once, but I think I've got a fan.

DOUBT: Or a stalker

GIGI: My *fan* is vibing my music! Wait, where's he – The club promoter, hands me a fifty. His clammy fingers slap my arse.

DOUBT: Reminding her why he really gave her the gig.

GIGI: I stop by the squat Polish cake shop, tucked away on a Soho side street. I'd love to say I wholeheartedly support this independent cafe, with their stale cakes and weird barista, but I'm only here because I get free tea.

DOUBT: Raff, the peculiar barista is trying to get into Gigi's pants. A fact she is fully aware of.

GIGI: I plonk myself on the beaten-up sofa and keep eye contact to a minimum "One milky tea with seven sugars please."

DOUBT: It's actually ten. Raff is, pun intended, sweet on Gigi. He's convinced himself his intentions are pure when in reality he probably just wants to fuck her

GIGI: Has the cosmic madness stopped? So far, things seem fine. Normal almost.

DOUBT: Doubt it

GIGI: It's over everyone! I've survived my Saturn's Return. It wasn't that bad.

PIPPIN: Gigi, it's 11 minutes past 11. It's got to be significant. Make a wish!

GIGI: I'm a bit fed up of empty wishes Pippin. I watch Raff bury chicken bones in the plant pot behind the till and pretend I haven't noticed.

PIPPIN: Can we find an edgier café please? This place isn't building traction on my TikTok

GIGI: Pippin shuffles further up my sleeve

DOUBT: Raff's looking extra deranged tonight. He stares at Gigi's tits and says;

RAFF: Your Chakras are out of balance. May I realign you?

DOUBT: As far as chat up lines go, it's original

GIGI: I'm good, thanks. Raff's taking the 'new age' hippy aesthetic a step too far. Barefoot, forever clutching crystals, he smells like wet dog. His hair is the texture of moss

DOUBT: Is he a man? Is he a tree? I'm not sure he knows

GIGI: He hands me my tea with an unexpected –

DOUBT: And unwanted / gift

GIGI: Gift

RAFF: I took it upon myself to pull you a Tarot card.

Gigi shows the audience a tarot card- it's The Tower.

The Tower is some heavy shit

GIGI: What the fuck does that mean?

DOUBT: It means he's praying on your vulnerability and using clever tactics to make you drop your knickers

GIGI: I stare at the card, panic rising, like a glitter cannon my limbs implode

Doubt throws confetti in a sarcastic way

Is this from Saturn's return?

DOUBT: Perhaps Raff's cast a spell, either way Gigi drops hot tea all down her front

GIGI: Instinct kicks in and I strip my blouse off

DOUBT: Raff does the same. Both semi naked and semi...

...

GIGI: What you done that for?

RAFF: I'm not entirely sure. I just follow my innate animal instincts.

GIGI: Is it me or is he covered in mud?

DOUBT: He's covered in mud.

GIGI: Raff hands me his jumper.

RAFF: I'd really like to help you. I need –

GIGI: I flee fast. What a shitty birthday.

DOUBT: Did you expect something different...? Gigi's about to do something incredibly stupid. She knows it's stupid and society will agree. Head in clouds, berating the day, she takes a wrong turn up a dicey alley where streetlamps don't exist

GIGI: Eternal darkness surrounds me

DOUBT: I would just like to illuminate that THIS is how the first character in every horror movie dies. Chopped into bite size pieces down an alley. ALONE. Remember, Gigi, you said you don't wanna join / the 27 Club

GIGI: The 27 Club. The hairs on my arms crawl to a stand

Weird noise

What was that?

DOUBT: Gigi?

GIGI: Yes

DOUBT: I think it's time to PANIC!!!!!!!!!

Doubt pulls an alarm. A classic warning alarm rings

GIGI: I'm running like something is chasing me

DOUBT: Because something IS chasing you!

GIGI: Doubt, this isn't helpful

DOUBT: Dark alleys are not your friend

GIGI: No shit Sherlock. I trip over a bin or a cat

DOUBT: Or maybe even a body!

GIGI: ARRGGGGHHHHHH!!!!!! This is not how I die!

DOUBT: Her face kisses the pavement

GIGI: I cling to the groove of a paving slab

DOUBT: I can taste the 27 Club!

GIGI: With one ferocious kick I whack, square in the face, whatever is mauling me.

DOUBT: Staring straight at her, are the red eyes of something inhuman. Teeth gnash hungrily

GIGI: This creature is gonna pounce

DOUBT: We're done for. We're dying! We're dying! Help! Do something!

GIGI: I open my mouth and:

I have to believe
This passion which burns inside
Will conquer not divide.
I'm destined to rise
I'm here to voice my words, worldwide.

The unearthly creature cocks its head and melts away

DOUBT: Rather unhelpfully, Gigi faints. Her head swims as her vision does the backstroke.

LUCIEN: Gigi...

DOUBT: Who the hell is that?

LUCIEN: It's alright, you're safe now

GIGI: Booms a voice as rich as double chocolate. Eyes so green they look like emeralds. A total fox in a suit. 6ft 2 and oozing charisma. If money had a smell, it would smell like him.

PIPPIN:	Golly gosh, he's dapper Gigi
LUCIEN:	I didn't mean to scare you
DOUBT:	Why are you chasing women down alleys then?
LUCIEN:	I've been trying to contact you
GIGI:	He slips me a business card. His pearly teeth dazzle. Teeth you only ever see in adverts. Or on Americans. Not real people
LUCIEN:	I was at your gig, and the one before. You have the most extraordinary talent. I'd love to help you. Call me…
GIGI:	He disappears into the night
	…
DOUBT:	…
PIPPIN:	Told you that wish would work! Perhaps fame is just around the corner
GIGI:	The next day I'm standing outside 666 Hell's Palace, Shoreditch. I caress the black card. Nothing but a first name, 'Lucien'. Utterly unGoogleable
DOUBT:	Pretty suspect if you ask me
GIGI:	A maze of never-ending corridors later and my feet meet a huge cast iron door with a brass angel-shaped handle.
PIPPIN:	What is this? Fifty Shades of Grey?

DOUBT: I'm inclined to agree

LUCIEN: Gigi Star! We're so glad you could make it. I've been singing, haha, your praises to everyone at Inferno. Did you find the place alright?..

GIGI: I...

LUCIEN: I just love your style. So quirky. Unique. Adorable...

GIGI: I can't muster a single word in this beautiful man's presence...

DOUBT: She isn't worthy

LUCIEN: Drink?

GIGI: A tall glass filled with what looks like salad, appears by magic

DOUBT: Looks like some bollocks Raff would drink

GIGI: I don't want to appear rude, so I sip

LUCIEN: You're a gifted performer, aren't you Gigi?

GIGI: Not sure if I'm supposed to nod in agreement –

DOUBT: Or be modestly British, so she blinks three times

Gigi blinks three times.

LUCIEN: You've not much traction online, with a talent like yours the world needs to know about it. What are your aspirations? Dreams? Goals?

DOUBT: Be able to pay her rent, stop inflation and survive her Saturn's return?

GIGI: Gold-plated records appear on the walls. Like a magpie my eyes latch on. The epitome of success

LUCIEN: At Inferno Records we only represent the best

GIGI: A crisp sheet of paper materialises. A quill appears in my palm. Sorry, is it me or is it hot in here?

DOUBT: His Cheshire cat smile curls at the edges. A heady, woozy feeling clouds her thoughts.

GIGI: What was in that drink?

PIPPIN: Salad, spirulina and a bit of kale

LUCIEN: Gigi, how about we make you the star your name implies? That piece of paper is a contract. A recording deal.. With Inferno Records you can perform for the rest of your life

GIGI: His words are soft as sugar syrup

DOUBT: Gigi, I'm not sure about this…

GIGI: Pippin scratches at the lining of my pocket. Four years slogging at temp jobs

PIPPIN: This is your moment

DOUBT: This is too good to be true

GIGI: Endless rejections

DOUBT: You don't deserve this

GIGI: A diet of 20p noodles, misery and sugar tea

DOUBT: What if it all goes tits up?

GIGI: This is all I've ever wanted served right here right now on a golden platter with salad

LUCIEN: It doesn't get better than this

DOUBT: The galaxy above twists and turns

Gigi looks at Doubt who shakes his head

GIGI: I sign on the dotted line

Musical interlude

DOUBT: It's time to take a hiatus from Gigi. No, not an interval. You will not be given the opportunity to leave and never return. While Gigi fantasises about her future, Raff is hyperventilating about his past

GIGI: Raff, in his dimly lit bedsit above the chicken shop on Peckham high street sniffs my blouse.

DOUBT: Like a complete weirdo. He wonders what shampoo she uses…

GIGI: Whatever's on offer. Herbal Essence. Coconut

DOUBT: He spots 'Gigi Star' sewn on the inside label of her top. What are you twelve?

GIGI: My mum did it

DOUBT: He checks her socials. Sees she's a singer – sort of. Reverberations from her music pulsate through

	his cells and his soul sparks. His chakras get all gooey and weird.
RAFF:	Gigi's it. She's the one to redress the balance

Music swells- replicating Raff's infatuation before-

GIGI:	HOLY SHIT EVERYTHING IS AMAZING WHEN YOU'RE (ALMOST) FAMOUS!
DOUBT:	Gigi has no idea what's going on, but her life has indeed transformed.
GIGI:	See! Admit it Doubt you were wrong. Inferno Records have given me so much
DOUBT:	Including chemically straightened hair. God forbid they'd ever cast a lead with curly hair.
GIGI:	Excuse me?
DOUBT:	Ever seen a female lead with curly hair?
GIGI:	No
DOUBT:	Curls are reserved for the ugly side characters

Awkward

	Gigi's given spray tans (plural)
GIGI:	A penthouse with an actual window. Pippin has his own room
PIPPIN:	But I prefer Gigi's sleeve. She's stopped wearing polyester. These new silks are doing wonders for my fur

GIGI: I've swapped Tinder for Raya

DOUBT: A wanky dating app for the 'elite'

GIGI: Cool, right?

DOUBT: Not really... After 'get ready for fame' training, Gigi is FINALLY in the studio

GIGI: It's happening!... Lucien, I've got some ideas for the debut. I'd love to show you

LUCIEN: We admire your dedication JooJoo

GIGI: It's Gigi

LUCIEN: Let's not get ahead of ourselves, eh? We've got to build a brand. Let's start with a few

Catchy but super naff shopping channel music:

ADVERT ONE:

> Tastes natural and good
> Just like you knew it would
> Got half fat
> But twice the fun
> Get this yoghurt in your tum
> Mountain yoghurt is my YUM
> Snack of choice. At only 90 calories it's a 'hmm' from me.

DOUBT: Weight loss only expected as part of a strict calorie-controlled diet. Please consult your doctor.

ADVERT TWO:

> You'll wonder where the yellow went
> When you brush your teeth with ColdaScent
> Gets rid of plaque and stains
> So minty fresh your man won't complain
> Pucker up baby it's kissing time
> With ColdaScent, Coldascent, ColdaScent- yeah.

ADVERT THREE:

> Bum, bum, bum, bum,
> Bum, bum, bum, bum, bum!
>
> RoidAway the cream for bum
> When Hemorrhoid's ruin your fun
>
> Booty magic, it's fantastic,
> Get your anus feeling elastic.
>
> Say goodbye to itchy pain!
> In your undies
> Lets get funsies!
> With everyone's favourite hemorrhoid cream.
>
> A little goes a long way
> RoidAway, putting the magic back into your day.

DOUBT: What the fuck is this shit?!

GIGI: All a bit weird but I'm grateful for the opportunity

DOUBT: Are you though?

GIGI: …

PIPPIN: You can't be performing advert jingles Gigi, this is proper shite

GIGI: It's just a stepping stone, Pippin. Career building

DOUBT: And here comes the self-help malarky

Gigi stands in a power pose

GIGI: I am on my way to becoming a world-famous artist. I am full of confidence and-

DOUBT: Bullshit. 66 days later, 11 minutes of standing in a power pose and Gigi finally grows some ovaries and asks Inferno Records;

GIGI: "Why am I performing terrible adverts selling terrible products?"

DOUBT: Lucien's eyes turn from green to red

GIGI: The same red as the eyes in the alley

LUCIEN: JooJoo, you're just not mainstream enough. We've done some data analysis

PIPPIN: What the bloody heck does that mean?

LUCIEN: Market research, focus groups and it turns out you're far too "authentic"

GIGI: Authenticity is good though, right?

LUCIEN: It's perfect! *You're* perfect

DOUBT: Is he gaslighting us?

LUCIEN: Which is why, we've decided, Satanic Advertising is where you belong. Selling products. You'll come to love it

PIPPIN: What fresh hell is this?

GIGI: Pippin drags the signed contract with his tail. Panic rises through my body

DOUBT: It wasn't this long when you signed it!

LUCIEN: Gigi Star, by signing this you hereby hand over your voice for eternity. You are in agreement that your vocal cords will become the sole property of Inferno Records and their sister company Satanic Advertising

GIGI: There's been some sort of mistake. But there in fine print, so small even Pippin needs a microscope:

GIGI/DOUBT: Satanic Advertising?

PIPPIN: For ETERNITY? Gigi that means forever! In case you haven't understood the gravitas of your predicament

Musical shift

GIGI: Everything's great! I've just been promoted. I'm now the voice of E.V!L – The infamous shopping channel

DOUBT: You should have read the small print...

GIGI: I'm trending on TikTok, right Pippin?

PIPPIN: I suppose

GIGI: With over 11 million views!

DOUBT: You're a meme

GIGI: How cool is that?

DOUBT: You're not moving people

GIGI: I'm happy

DOUBT: Are you?

GIGI: I'm rich!

DOUBT: What will all five hundred occupants of Hummel Doddie think?

GIGI: They'll think I'm a success

DOUBT: You're kidding yourself and the adverts have gotten awful sinister

GIGI: Not all of them. I've just finished recording for a big charity

DOUBT: Who support conversion therapy

GIGI: …

DOUBT: And are anti-abortion

GIGI: You can say what you want Doubt, but I'm not listening

Doubt breaks out into song

DOUBT: Sell out
I told you I'm here for a purpose
My existence is to make you nervous.

You're a sell out girl
My message may be unkind
But baby, I'm all in your mind

Underneath the money and memes
Is a pit of unfilled dreams
Don't let them fester
Or they'll grow
To the size of Moscow

GIGI: Doubt's right. I don't want to be recording adverts. I want to be recording real music, with real lyrics

PIPPIN: Perhaps it's worth talking to Lucien again. Try and break your contract?

GIGI: It's worth a shot

DOUBT: She arrives at 666 Hells Palace only to find it's disappeared. Lucien won't return her calls

GIGI: Or E-mails

DOUBT: WhatsApps

GIGI: Blackberry Pings

DOUBT: MSN messages

GIGI: Letters

DOUBT: Pigeons

GIGI: It's no good, Pippin. I've messed up

DOUBT: She weeps into her pocket, where Pippin tries not to drown

PIPPIN: Let's run away, Gigi!

DOUBT: Gigi's schedule shows no sign of letting up, until she hits 35 when they debate how sellable she is, being geriatric

GIGI: At least I've been granted leave for my Nana's 90th birthday in Hummel Doddie

Musical interlude

With weary feet I pass the squat polish cake shop. My heart yearns to sit on their beaten-up sofa just for a moment of normality. I spy Raff staring into the distance and wonder what goes on in that strange head of his

DOUBT: He cleanses crystals and whispers to the moon. He's seen Gigi's commercials and they make his skin crawl. But something about her has gotten under his crawling skin. I suspect lust play's a large part. He looks like soft boy and probably is

RAFF: I read cosmic energy

DOUBT: Raff's intense nature comes from the turmoil of having a drunken mother and an abusive stepfather. At only 24, he is a secret assassin

RAFF: I'm what you might call a fugitive

DOUBT: When Raff was 14, he accidentally blew up his parents, but seeing as they weren't all that great in the parental department perhaps it wasn't as accidental as he thought...

RAFF: I lurk in the shadows of this oversaturated city with all the other forgotten people. I was raised by deer in a forest where no one could hear my screams. My connection to the universe is way beyond my years... Being a Virgo helps... Which is worse? To feel like you have no purpose or to have purpose but no means to fulfil it? I wonder what Gigi is doing with hers.

GIGI: I'm so excited to be home!

DOUBT: Mr and Mrs Star don't mention how their daughter has halved in size. They say nothing, because they're English

GIGI: Everything's great. I was overreacting. I just needed a break. Happy 90th birthday Nana!! At the Doddie Arms everyone's so happy to see me

DOUBT: Everyone's judging you

GIGI: Everyone's gagging to hear how I've conquered London. "It's going well, yeah"

DOUBT: Is it though?

GIGI: I'm recording all the time

DOUBT: Someone shoves a mic in Gigi's hand "Sing Gigi! For your nana!"

GIGI: I – Sorry. I can't – I'm contractually bound to Inferno Records and their sister company Satanic Advertising

DOUBT: Awkward...

GIGI: I feel like a dickhead

DOUBT: You sound like a dickhead. Looks like you've gotten too big for your boots. Pippin's drunk on ginger ale and fat with stodgy tea cake

PIPPIN: Lucien's never going to know, is he?

GIGI: Pippin, you raise a good point

DOUBT: I'm beginning to feel a bit panicky

GIGI: It's for Nana! She's 90! Come on.

DOUBT: She says the two most powerful yet dangerous words anyone can ever say...

GIGI: Fuck it

With a mic in hand
I feel my soul expand.
For the first time in months
I'm getting goosebumps.
Soaring like an eagle
Devoid of all evil.
Just pure love and connection.

> I have to believe,
> This passion which burns inside
> Will conquer not divide.
> I'm destined to rise
> I'm here to voice my words, worldwide.

LUCIEN: Gigi Star, you are in breach of your contract

DOUBT: This isn't good!

GIGI: What's happening? A gust of fire heads straight towards me

LUCIEN: Your voice belongs to ME!

DOUBT: The flames mould into the shape of a pitchfork and wrap themselves around Gigi's throat

GIGI: Help!

LUCIEN: Did you really think you could betray me?!!! Fool ME?!!!

PIPPIN: Gigi, run!!

DOUBT: It's too late. With one stab, he plucks her vocal cords. As quickly as he arrived, Lucien leaves with Gigi's voice

Musical interlude

GIGI: It's been a week. I sit on a decaying sofa on the roof of the warehouse where I used to live

DOUBT: Her windowless room already occupied by some other poor soul

GIGI: I've never felt so lost

DOUBT: She gazes at the stars above. Their shimmery magic, fading in this cruel city. Gigi can still speak, sort of, but her voice is a hoarse whisper

GIGI: What am I going to do? Performing was my identity. It's all I am, it's all I want

DOUBT: Gigi? Perhaps it wasn't meant to be

GIGI: Don't say that

DOUBT: It hasn't worked out

GIGI: Things aren't supposed to be easy

DOUBT: Are they meant to be this hard?

GIGI: It's Saturn's Return, if I survive this then –

DOUBT: It wasn't working out before then. There comes a point when you've just got to grow up. You tried and it didn't work…

GIGI: Is there no reward for individuality?
This industry praises cookie cutter personality
Over authenticity. Difference.
Is there really no place for someone like me?
All I ask for is a seat at the table
Not to be labelled as some commercial commodity,
Another wannabe
To Increase the Devil's economy.

DOUBT: Gigi… Forget performing. Go back to Hummel Doddie and start again.

GIGI: I can't return. My roots have grown cold
Their strength covered in mould
Which festers at the thought of going home
I'm a fable of failure.
I've let them all down.

PIPPIN: Gigi, home is wherever you make it. You don't need to go back.

GIGI: Music was my home. I'm nothing but a body without a purpose

A circus without an act.
I have to let it go,
Now nothing but a distant memory.
Collecting dust in the corner of my mind
Like a broken antique.
Or a child's toy, discarded, left behind
Dissolving into past
Like a faded picture
Of times gone by.
All colours – drained

DOUBT: She watches a shooting star catapult towards its demise. Halfway across town Raff stares at that same star on his smoking break

RAFF: I don't smoke, but it's the only way to get a break from washing dishes

DOUBT: Since meeting Gigi everything has felt funny – both in his loins and in his soul. He ponders his predicament

RAFF: I've got to redress the balance between light and dark or my karma is, like, properly fucked

DOUBT: He maps Gigi's face amongst the polluted stars and asks the universe to provide a means of redemption:

RAFF: It's time to leverage joy and abolish guilt. Gigi Star, show yourself

Gigi takes a deep breath, as if something has hit her chest. She pulls out the tarot card and stares at it

GIGI: Sugar tea

Actor rings café bell

RAFF: What the fuck. The universe actually answered my call. When we stop obsessing about our desires that's usually when we get them

Gigi holds up the Tarot Card

GIGI: What does this mean?

RAFF: The Tower card means chaos and upheaval

GIGI: My life is a mess

DOUBT: He nods as if to say he knew that already

GIGI: Are you some sort of wizard?

RAFF: No, not really

DOUBT: He hands Gigi a sugar tea with a slice of red velvet cake

RAFF: For your pet mouse

PIPPIN: I'm not a pet, I'm a companion… How does he know about me, Gigi?

GIGI: He stares *at* me, *through* me. Is he-

DOUBT: High or just a raving lunatic?

GIGI: His earth-coloured eyes meet my ocean blues and out of nowhere, I –

DOUBT: Please don't cry

GIGI: Sob and snot all over him

DOUBT: Stop, this is embarrassing

RAFF: This is gonna sound properly mental but I'm like, destined to help you. Karmically.

DOUBT: Code for, I'm gonna shag you then blame our star sign incompatibility for the reason I stop returning your calls

RAFF: And my guides are telling me, you're my calling card

GIGI: Guides? Calling card?

RAFF: I've done some bad shit, which I need to set right

DOUBT: We said no more bad boys. You cannot be the one to turn them good

GIGI: But what if he can help me? I'm desperate

DOUBT: You're not *that* desperate

GIGI: Stop the music. [stage manager's name], can you bring the house lights up?

House lights up.

You've got to let me breathe. Make mistakes, take risks.

DOUBT: I'm protecting you. I'm just trying to keep you safe

GIGI: You're trying to keep me comfortable. There's no growth in comfort. I can't do this with you constantly holding me back.

DOUBT: Fine, but are you ready? Are you worth it?...

...

Are you?

GIGI: Yes. I am worth it

DOUBT: I don't believe you

Gigi puts an elastic band on her wrist.

Then I will train you to. Every time you act out this is getting snapped.

Gigi pulls the elastic band. Doubt and Gigi flinch in pain

OUCH!

GIGI: [stage manager's name] dim the lights

Stage lights on

	Raff, my music voice was stolen. Doubt is creeping in and making me think I'm not worth it. Maybe Doubt's right, maybe I'm not cut out for this industry, but somewhere deep inside I do think performing is what I'm meant to do, I'm just – I'm lost.
DOUBT:	Raff, holds her hand and tries to stop his blood travelling south.
RAFF:	I don't know if our purpose is pre-decided or if we choose, but I wanna help you get your voice back. Where is it?
DOUBT:	If we knew that we'd get it ourselves.

Gigi pulls the elastic band

W/GIGI:	OUCH!
GIGI:	Lucien from Inferno Records stole it.
RAFF:	Lucien? As in Lucifer? As in…
GIGI:	Admitting I signed a contract with the Devil sounds ridiculous.
RAFF:	Right. Well… we better write a list.
GIGI:	You a Virgo by any chance?
RAFF:	With a Taurus rising and Libra Moon
DOUBT:	Well, that's a – (*Gigi threatens to silence him*) Could be worse
GIGI:	His list consists of colanders

DOUBT:	Pots
GIGI:	Pans
DOUBT:	And rolls and rolls and rolls of tin foil
GIGI:	Why?
RAFF:	Trust me. We've got Mother Earth on our side
GIGI:	I don't have a clue what he's on about but despite the fact he smells odd, doesn't wear shoes and gazes randomly at my –
DOUBT:	[Tits] *Gigi pulls the elastic* Ouch!
GIGI:	Chakras. I'm sort of…
DOUBT:	Once you say it you can't take it back
GIGI:	Finding him quite attractive
PIPPIN:	Bloody hell, not this again, Gigi.
GIGI:	He wants to help
DOUBT:	Does he? Or is he just another soft boy pretending to be a feminist when in reality he's just another piece in the patriarchy… OUCH!!!
GIGI:	Doubt, reign in the cynicism. It's exhausting

Raff eyeballs Gigi

RAFF:	Scorpio, right?
GIGI:	Scorpio – Sagittarius cusp
RAFF:	That's a lot of feelings. I know what you need.

DOUBT: To get her vocal cords back?

RAFF: Gigi, you ain't gonna get very far if you're carrying the weight of him on your shoulders *(he indicates Doubt)*.

DOUBT: How can he see me?

RAFF: We're all just energy, but Doubt's a terrible thing. It'll grow like fungus and eat you alive. It's time to lighten your negative baggage.

GIGI: I've started

She snaps her elastic band

DOUBT: Ouch!... I'm feeling attacked from all sides

RAFF: It's time we start our quest.

Musical interlude

GIGI: We arrive in Hastings

PIPPIN: I suspect Lucien doesn't live here

DOUBT: London snobbery oozes from Pippin's paws.

GIGI: Raff... Why do you want to help me?

DOUBT: He shifts awkwardly scratching at the dirt on his skin

RAFF: I killed my parents, went on the run, and was raised by a group of deer

DOUBT: Alright Bear Grylls

RAFF:	The deer told me if I want to find peace, I have to remedy the terrible things I've done.
GIGI:	And there I was thinking he liked me
RAFF:	I figure helping you will rebalance my life. Also, I think you're fit
GIGI:	Score
RAFF:	I know you think I'm weird and you was just using me for free tea, but I'm not just some new age dickhead. I do actually care
GIGI:	I feel guilty for judging him
DOUBT:	I still think he's full of shit - OUCH! Okay, okay, sorry.
RAFF:	We should press on. Wind is shifting
PIPPIN:	Gigi, why are we standing in a field of bluebells?
GIGI:	I take in the wonders of a huge forest opening… Raff, where are we?
RAFF:	Home
PIPPIN:	I am not living in a forest Gigi
GIGI:	The trees bend and curve magically
PIPPIN:	Open space makes me anxious.
RAFF:	I need you to stay very still
GIGI:	Suddenly the clearing is flooded with wildlife. Badgers, foxes, rabbits, the lot.

DOUBT: Even I have to admit this is magical. A beautiful deer makes its way to Raff.

GIGI: Raff outstretches his palm, and the deer embraces it. Pippin rustles in my frizzy hair

PIPPIN: That thing is going to eat me, isn't it?

DOUBT: Raff and the deer nod at each other for what feels like eternity.

Actor nods a few times in awkward silence

RAFF: The animals have offered to help

DOUBT: How's that going to work?

RAFF: You have to perform

GIGI: I can't

RAFF: You can still perform in your heart

DOUBT: …

RAFF: If there's magic in your words they'll hear it, Gigi.

GIGI: I figure he's got me this far...

DODDIE 1: "Don't forget us!"

DODDIE 2: "Do Hummel Doddie proud!"

GIGI: I breathe in, feel into my cells
Recalling simpler times.
When colours stayed within the lines
Not spilling out in Chaos.

A woman's voice is a powerful thing,
No wonder he stripped me down
Morphed me into a silent clown.

If only I could perform again
Remembering how it felt before the downward spiral
Of London crept into my bones.

Before greed seeped into my veins.
Transformed into marketing campaigns,
Void of all joy and honesty.

A fool to look at
A lock without a key
A tree without leaves
Just a carcass which grieves and laments for a lost purpose.

I have to believe,
This passion which burns inside
Will conquer not divide.
I'm destined to rise
I'm here to voice my words, worldwide.

DOUBT: The animals stand transfixed and weep

PIPPIN: Gigi, you did it!

GIGI: Raff collects their tears in a tiny hip flask.

DOUBT: Who under the age of 50 carries a hip flask?

PIPPIN: I'm kind of into it

RAFF: We should rest

DOUBT: Here? Really?

GIGI: Raff hugs me close as we settle down to sleep

DOUBT: Is this safe? Alone in the middle of a forest

GIGI: Think of it as glamping just without the glamour or tent.

PIPPIN: Gigi, I'll just be over here, next to this rather attractive fieldmouse.

GIGI: Classic

RAFF: The badgers have been digging a tunnel all night.

PIPPIN: Please don't tell me we're going down there

RAFF: This'll lead to us Hell

DOUBT: Did he just say Hell? Is he taking the piss?

GIGI: We'll burn to a crisp down there!

PIPPIN: What's the point of this junk?

RAFF: Gifts. From the animals.

DOUBT: It's a random collection of stuff. Antlers, turtle shells, moth wings.

GIGI: Raff, why are you wrapping us in aluminium foil?

Gigi and Doubt put on silver capes and colanders for helmets

DOUBT: We look ridiculous

RAFF: We look like legends

PIPPIN: We look like jacket potatoes, ready for the oven. Is this nonsense to protect us from 5G?

RAFF: No, the flames of Hell, obviously. You'll be needing this £1 coin

DOUBT: They set foot down the tunnel.

PIPPIN: Christ, I didn't sign up for this!

GIGI: It's just a bit of dirt Pippin.

DOUBT: I don't mean to alarm you, Gigi, but you've got three days left to survive your Saturn's return. So, perhaps entering a tunnel which leads to Hell, is not the best idea.

GIGI: Doubt, you were doing so well

Music stops

PIPPIN: What's happening?...

GIGI: My insides somersault

RAFF: There should be a boat.

Raff raises his coin

Entry fee

GIGI: Is that the River Thames?

DOUBT: I think it's supposed to be River Styx

GIGI: Then why does it look like the Thames? Are you kidding me? We've just trekked all this way to be back at the foot of the Thames.

DOUBT: That's no ordinary Thames.

GIGI: English GCSE flashes before my eyes

DOUBT: River Styx is full of secrets and past mistakes. If you enter the water, old regrets will consume you

...

I just had to tell you that.

GIGI: Perhaps I'd be better off finding my purpose as a silent nun.

RAFF: Gigi! Stop! We need your vocals to show the world that the underdog can make a difference. We must rise against capitalism. Unite for all the voiceless, for all those who feel powerless in the face of exploitation. How can we find peace whilst others suffer?!"

DOUBT: Alright Braveheart

RAFF: And I don't wanna be reincarnated as a worm. So, we have to get your vocals back, alright?

GIGI: There's no way across.

PIPPIN: You lot never think laterally. So much for being creatives. These gifts should do the trick

GIGI: We set sail in three turtle shells after a somewhat traumatic float test.

Doubt huffs and puffs drenched in water

DOUBT: I don't want to talk about it

	River Styx, AKA The Thames, begins to work her mischief.
PIPPIN:	Close your eyes, Gigi!
GIGI:	There in the depths of the murky London water lie the faces of Hummel Doddie.
DOUBT:	Their eyes so full of disappointment.
DODDIE 1:	"You forgot us!"
DODDIE 2:	"You didn't do Hummel Doddie proud!"
GIGI:	They really do think I'm a sell-out
PIPPIN:	Don't touch the water, Raff!
DOUBT:	Raff weeps as he watches how he blew up his parents. The haunting of his past tugs heavy on his guilty heart.
GIGI:	Pippin, what do you see?
PIPPIN:	Sweet fuck all my darling, my life is a blessing.
GIGI:	With apparently zero life regrets, Pippin lobs his £1 coin at Raff
RAFF:	Ow!!
PIPPIN:	Snap out of it, eco boy!
GIGI:	He covers my eyes with his paws. My pain makes his whiskers shiver.
PIPPIN:	You simply must let go of this self-indulgent guilt, Gigi. Honestly, life's not that important.

GIGI: Bit ironic as we head towards Hell

PIPPIN: Bet we'll find the Devil where the sun sets.

Musical moment.

GIGI: We head West, through a scorched landscape. Not ideal when dressed head to toe in tinfoil

RAFF: I will not tolerate this slander against our ingenious protection suits

Both actors' slowly roll eyes upwards

GIGI: What in the name of God?...

DOUBT: Is that Cerberus?! The three headed dog guarding the gateway to Hell

CERBERUS: GOD?! Who's speaking such blasphemy? Eh?

PIPPIN: ME!

CERBERUS: Oiiiii, Lads, lads, lads, lads, lads! Come on England!

DOUBT: Cerberus is a British Bulldog? He glares with all six eyes.

PIPPIN: He absolutely stinks of Heineken and sweat

CERBERUS: You hooligans *alive?*

PIPPIN: Can we get past please?

CERBERUS: You lot think you can just cross River Styx, come 'ere and take our jobs. Where you lot from then?

DOUBT: Oh Jesus Christ, he's one of them

CERBERUS: You a Jesus worshipper? Well, you lot can get back in your boats and piss off.

GIGI: It's a flying visit

CERBERUS: Who d'you support?

DOUBT: He cannot be serious

GIGI: Not really into football

PIPPIN: Arsenal!!!!!!

CERBERUS: Arsenal?! Aston Villa all the way!

PIPPIN: How do we get past?

CERBERUS: What's a pretty girl like you doing down here anyways? Cheer up, love!

GIGI: Nice to see misogyny still exists, even underground

DOUBT: We're in Hell, Gigi. Expect everything awful to be amplified. And just when it can't get any worse, he lifts up his hind leg and pisses all over Raff

RAFF: Not quite the spiritual awakening I've been seeking

CERBERUS: To pass, you must answer my riddle correctly...

DOUBT: Please don't be about football

CERBERUS: What can be lost, but never returned?

Actors look at the audience...

DOUBT: Anyone?

CERBERUS: You get three guesses

DOUBT: Hope it's not her vocal cords.

CERBERUS: TWO guesses!

GIGI: That was a sarcastic guess, from the negative part of my ego, it doesn't count!

CERBERUS: I said TWO guesses!

GIGI: Anyone know what can be lost but never returned?

Actors egg on a few audience members - improvising for a bit

PIPPIN: Psst. Think I've got it, Gigi. The answer is "Life"

CERBERUS: POOAARRRR! You've only gone and got right. That's a shame, I was starting to enjoy your company. Even if you are dirty Gooners. Oi, Oi!

DOUBT: Can we press on now please? In a bit of a hurry.

CERBERUS: What was that? Nah, think I've changed my mind. Gets lonely down here. Just me and my toxic masculinity. I'd like some Com-Pannny! Com-Panny!

PIPPIN: Gigi?

GIGI: Yeah?

PIPPIN: I suggest we…

GIGI: /RUUU**NNNNNNNNN**!!!!

DOUBT: /RUUU**NNNNNNNNN**!!!!

GIGI: Escaping the literal jaws of Hell, has given me a stitch... I don't mean to alarm anyone, but I think I'm stuck

'On hold' music begins:

PIPPIN: Right you are, I think we might be on hold Gigi

DOUBT: This really is Hell

GIGI: Raff? You alright?

RAFF: Hmm. Meditating. Ommmmm

DOUBT: Three hours later and we finally get through

GIGI: Don't get too excited. Looks like we're in Ikea

Actors shudder

PIPPIN: Just follow the arrows toward the exit

RAFF: I think there's a shortcut

DOUBT: No!! It's an Ikea trap. Their shortcuts never work

GIGI: After rows of ugly sofas, lamps and cheap smelling candles we finally reach the exit.

A load of Tupperware and their lids falls from the ceiling

What are we supposed to do with all this?

RAFF: I'm really not big on plastic

DOUBT: Seeing as we're in Hell, I'm assuming these containers need their rightful lids put on.

GIGI: I think that might be the only useful thing you've said so far

They frantically put the lids on all the Tupperware

PIPPIN: Gigi, look over there.

GIGI: Right up ahead in the Belly of Hades is Lucien

DOUBT: What do we do now?

RAFF: We need all the elements to defeat him. Gigi – Water. Me – Earth, Lucien – Fire. We need air

PIPPIN: Erm, hello. I'm an Aquarius. Thanks for asking.

GIGI: Why's he pickled my vocals in a glass jar?

DOUBT: He lusts for their power.

PIPPIN: Think of the all the wrong he can do with your voice, Gigi. He's already used you to make himself rich. What's next? He'll use the magic of your voice to hypnotise and make everyone believe they're worthless. To remove their free will. He will strip the world of human rights and remove all creativity. He will silence others as he's silenced you

GIGI: What's the plan then?

Raff shrugs

	All this and there's no plan? Raff, do something with your chakras or your crystals
DOUBT:	Told you Raff was chatting shit
RAFF:	Spirituality doesn't work like that. There comes a point when you've got to take action
DOUBT:	What's the action then?
RAFF:	Grab them!!
GIGI:	Lucien throws a fireball!
RAFF:	Ah, not my cape… ARGH!! My thigh looks like a lump of charcoal
DOUBT:	Pippin climbs up Lucien's leg.
LUCIEN:	Get off me you rodent!!
GIGI:	In all the kerfuffle Lucien releases the jar. The sole purpose of my life is suspended in mid air
PIPPIN:	Two hands Gigi!
DOUBT:	Hey, Gigi?
GIGI:	Not now, Doubt
DOUBT:	It's time for me to go.
GIGI:	What?
DOUBT:	You've done it. You were right, you don't need me.
GIGI:	Don't go

DOUBT: Why not?

GIGI: You're my safety blanket. We're friends

DOUBT: You've got better friends now.

GIGI: And with that I catch the jar. Just as Doubt runs into the fiery flames

PIPPIN: For goodness sake

GIGI: Pippin ties a pair of moth wings around his shiny foiled middle and beats his wings. His tail wrapped around the hipflask of tears. It's a hell of a thing to see a flying mouse wrapped in tin foil...

PIPPIN: Guard those cords with your life, Gigi! And for Christ's sake, perform for the love of it, never for fame!

GIGI: Pippin, NO!!! ... Like a literal moth to a flame, he flies into the heart of danger. With skill and finesse his tail unscrews the cap and he throws the contents into the eyes of the Devil, the gateway to his soul.

LUCIEN: ARRRRRGGGGGGHHHHHH!!!!!!!!!!!!!

GIGI: The compassion from the animal's tears burns Lucien's retinas. His satanic spirit sizzles

LUCIEN: You can't defeat me

GIGI: In blind rage Lucien accidentally sets himself on fire.

PIPPIN: Greed destroying itself as per usual

GIGI: But in a final fit of fury, Lucien grabs hold of Pippin –

PIPPIN: Gigi!!!!

GIGI: No!!! He crushes Pippin's tiny torso in his giant fist. Dust amongst the flames

Eulogy music

Unbeknownst to me, Pippin was experiencing his own Saturn's Return. He was a mouse of the people. An agent of change. Audience member number four, open your envelope please.

Audience member four opens envelope

FOUR: Pippin

GIGI: RIP – I guess he was always destined for the 27 Club. My life's purpose meant more to him than his own life.

I muster the strength to drag Raff back to the forest. Turns out there was a lift. All that trekking when we could have just taken the bloody lift. I feel terrible. Haunted by guilt. It's my fault Pippin has gone.

Doubt returns as Conviction

CONVICTION: No, it isn't

GIGI: And it's my fault Raff's leg looks like it's been left on the barbeque too long. My heart aches... Doubt! You're back... You seem different

CONVICTION: Figured I was due an upgrade. Like a phoenix, I rose from the ashes and emerged as... Conviction

GIGI: Looks good on you

CONVICTION: Thank you...

GIGI: Raff hasn't opened his eyes for hours. I'm sorry, I never meant to cause him pain.

CONVICTION: The animals surround them and with a gentle nod from the deer, Gigi curls up and sleeps. Praying things will be better come morning.

Musical interlude

In the dead of night, the bees coat Raff's burns with healing honey and royal jelly. The cats lick their wounds clean. And after some very delicate and intricate surgery, silkworms stitch Gigi's vocal cords back into their rightful place... They begin to stir, their heartbeats harmonising with the break of dawn.

RAFF: Gigi... We're alive! Has it worked? Can you perform?

GIGI: I'm a bit scared to try. All my voice has brought is chaos and grief. My heart feels heavy. My dungarees' pocket so empty and cold.

CONVICTION: I believe in you Gigi... Try

How lucky we are to have survived,
To be alive
To have found each other.
I got so caught up in chasing fame
That I forgot to maintain what really matters.
Pippin was right.
We only get one life,
So do what ignites your soul.
Success comes in many forms.
Life's about weathering the storm
And trusting that you can't have sun without shade.
Even when Mercury is in retrograde
It's possible for doubt to upgrade to conviction
There's always a reason to count your lucky stars.
Because now I believe,
This passion which burns inside
Will conquer not divide.
I'm destined to rise
I'm here to voice my words, worldwide.

The animals weep, bow and one by one begin to disappear back into the thick of the forest...

GIGI: Raff, Are those little stumps growing out of your forehead or is my Saturn's Return playing up again?

CONVICTION: He definitely has stumpy horns

RAFF: Finally! My initiation has begun! It worked. I've redressed the karmic balance. Rewritten my wrongs and I'm ready to rejoin my deer family.

CONVICTION: Is he saying he's part deer?

GIGI: I think so, yeah... Kind of into it, kind of suits him.
We head to the sea and sit quietly,
Drunk on the sobriety of what we've been through.
An inner calm and newfound gratitude,
A change in attitude.

Raff, I don't think London's for me. It's exhausting, no-one smiles, and I really like windows.

RAFF: I hate the bedsit above the chicken shop on Peckham high street and technically I stole all those utensils from the cake shop. So, I don't think I can return.

CONVICTION: So, they stay. In Hastings. Raff runs an eco-friendly coffee shop, so bougie Pippin would have approved. And Gigi plays in a successful band.

GIGI: Now that I make music for love, not fame, people hear the magic.

CONVICTION: Gigi and Raff date for a bit but decide it's just weird.

GIGI: What with Raff spending more and more time with his deer family and me performing, it isn't meant to be.

CONVICTION: Gigi has survived her Saturn's Return everyone! Wooo! Round of applause please!

Doubt gets audience to clap

GIGI: Finally!!!

CONVICTION: Just in time for the chaos of your thirties

GIGI: Don't

CONVICTION: She finally knows who she is. She's escaped the endless series of boxes inside boxes. No straightened hair, no spray tans (plural) and no pretence. Just Gigi Star

GIGI: And my Vocal Cords of Magic.

The End.